Get With It!

101-PLUS Pop Culture Idioms *and* Expressions

Harry Collis
Illustrated by Joe Kohl

Alta Book Center Publishers
www.altaesl.com

Cover and Interior Illustrations: Joe Kohl

Acquisitions Editor: Aaron Almendares-Berman
Lead Content Editor: Jamie Cross

The publisher acknowledges Jon Jensen, Simón Almendares-Berman, and Jeremy Walker for their keen editorial insights and review.

Author's Acknowledgements
It is with deep emotion and pride that I gratefully acknowledge the input of my grandsons, Adam Jennison and Nicholas Metcalfe, in the writing of this book. Their guidance and suggestions proved invaluable in assuring that both the expressions and the situations compiled in the text reflect current cultural thought.

My other grandsons, Jack Metcalfe, and Mark, Alex, and Joseph Jennison, were also integral contributors. They kept their "bubba" immersed in pop culture and were always at the ready when I needed a suggestion or scenario.

My profound appreciation also goes out to my editors, Jamie Cross and Jon Jensen, for their insightful suggestions and revisions.

Alta Book Center Publishers
www.altaesl.com

ISBN: 978-1-932383-15-7
Library of Congress Control Number: 2007934711

Contents

Foreword   v

Section 1   1
It's Up to You: *Idioms for taking action*
the Ball's in Your Court • to Roll • to Get With It
to Get the Lead Out • to Stay On One's Toes
to Be Up to Something • to Have Something Up One's Sleeve
to Be Game • You're On • to Take a Crack at Something
to Head Out • Let's Blow This Joint • to Knock It Off
to Stick Up for Someone • Wrap It Up

Section 2   19
Keep Your Pants On: *Idioms for a hectic life*
to Take a Rain Check • to Be Tied Up • to Be Over One's Head
to Not Have a Clue • Beats Me • to Be Stumped • to Be Done
to Be Beat • Cannot Hack It • to Be Burned Out
to Be On Edge • to Get Carried Away • to Get Out of Hand
to Fly Off the Handle • to Freak Out • to Be Pissed Off
to Blow Up • to Go Bananas • to Go Off the Deep End
to Hit the Ceiling • to Be Trippin' • to Be Out of Whack
to Get a Grip • to Hang In There • to Lay Off
to Lighten Up • to Give Someone a Break

Section 3   49
Taking Care of Business: *Idioms for assuming responsibility*
to Call the Shots • to Get the Ball Rolling • to Start From Scratch
to Pull Something Off • to Give It a Go/Shot/Whirl
to Take the Heat • to Go to Bat for Someone • to Come Clean
to Fill Someone In • to Be No Big Deal • to Be a Piece of Cake
to Get the Hang of (It) • to Nail Something (Down)
to Put (Something) On the Back Burner • to Cough up

Section 4   67
Let the Good Times Roll: *Idioms for good fortune*
Way to Go • to Have It Made • to Have a Blast/Ball
to Be Up One's Alley • to Be On a Roll • to Be Sweet
to Be Tight • to Be Hot • to Be Hooked (On)
to Hook Someone Up • to Hit On Someone
to Dig (Someone or Something) • to Knock Someone Dead
Knock Yourself Out • to Die For • to Rock

Section 5   85
What Happened? *Idioms for delivering bad news*
to Blow It/Something • to Do a Number On Someone/Something
to Be Wasted • to Be Busted • to Be Caught Red-Handed
to Get Ripped Off/to Be a Rip Off • to Get the Short End of the Stick
to Have a Falling Out • to Have a Bone to Pick with Someone
to Have It In for Someone • to Let Someone Have It
to Give Someone a Hard Time • to Throw In the Towel
to Shake Up Someone • to Give It to Someone Straight
to Be a Bummer • to Be Bummed Out • to Let Someone Down
to Be a Drag • to Suck • to Mess/Screw Up • to Be Screwed
to Be/Skate On Thin Ice • In Your Face • to Chicken Out (On)

Section 6   113
That's Life: *Idioms for everything else*
What's Up (with Somebody)? • to Chill Out • to Tag Along
to Go Dutch • to Crash (Someplace) • to Mess/Screw Around
to Keep In Touch • to Stick to One's Guns • No Way (José)
Screw That • Go Figure • to Butt In • to Rub It In
That Cracks Me Up

Idioms Index   129

Foreword

Given that language is in a constant state of flux from one generation to another, words and expressions that reflect the culture of the younger generation are soon dispersed throughout the general population. Native speakers, young and old, incorporate these expressions into their daily speech and, thus, the expressions become an integral part of the language.

It is no surprise that for non-native speakers these "additions" to the language may well constitute a barrier for the comprehension of not only the language but also for some facets of American culture and mores.

Get With It! is designed to provide the newcomer to American English with an insight into many of the words and expressions now a part of contemporary American speech, thus providing an avenue for assimilation into the native culture of America.

Get With It! is divided into six sections, each section containing items reflecting the focal point of the title of that section. The manual is meant to be a "fun book" enabling the reader to gain easy access to the language that can open the door to contemporary American thought.

Section One

It's Up to You

Idioms for taking action

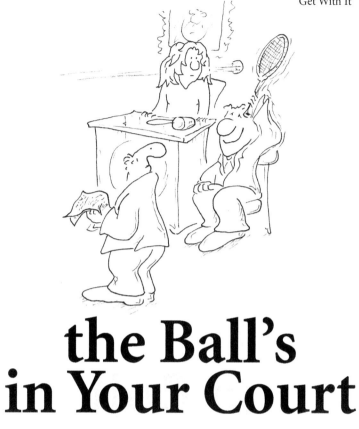

the Ball's in Your Court

it's your turn to take action

- Look, we found you a great lawyer. Now **the ball's in your court**. It's up to you to tell the jury exactly what happened. *Take action* and you'll win the case!

- You could easily sell your baseball card collection for a lot of money. **The ball's in your court** (*it's your turn to take action*).

to Roll

to get going; to start

- "Hey, **let's roll** or we'll be late for class."
  "Okay. *Let's get going!*"

- "You want to keep your dog-walking business going, don't you?"
  "Of course!"
  "Well then, let's **get rolling** (*get started*)! We've got ten more poodles to walk before sunset."

poodles: dogs with long, curly hair

to Get With It

to modernize one's attitudes and behavior; to take action to do what others do; to hurry up

- Why are you wearing that outdated t-shirt? **Get with it** and *start wearing more modern, up-to-date clothes!* You don't want your friends to think that you don't know the latest trends, do you?

- Come on! **Get with it** (*jump in and join the fun*)! Every one is in the swimming pool, and you're just sitting there all alone in the corner.

outdated: not popular
latest trends: most popular styles of clothing

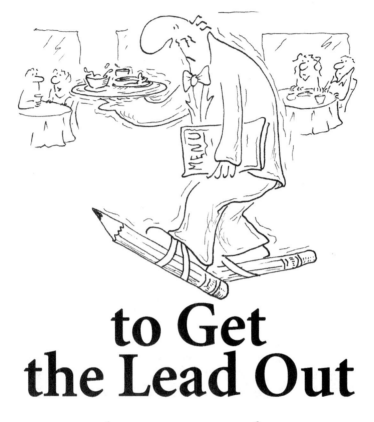

to Get the Lead Out

to hurry up; to move faster

- Service in this restaurant is too slow. The waiters need to **get the lead out.** If they don't *hurry up,* they're going to lose my business!

- What are you guys standing around for? Come on! **Get the lead out** (*move faster*)! We've got to finish setting up before the ceremony starts!

setting up: getting everything ready

to Stay
On One's Toes

to be ready to react; to notice things at all times

- One has **to stay on one's toes** in the world of fashion. One day mini skirts are in, the next day they're out. That's why I read all the latest fashion magazines *to stay informed of the latest trends.*

- You should **stay on your toes** (*notice things at all times*) in this part of town. Crime is rampant in this neighborhood.

are in: are in style/fashion
are out: are out of style/fashion
trends: styles/fashions
rampant: growing

to Be Up to Something

to be acting suspiciously;
to be secretly planning something

- I wonder what that guy **is up to**. He's been hanging around here all morning and he's *acting suspiciously.*

- "Why are Gil and Ryan whispering in the back of the room?"
  "I bet **they're up to something** (*planning to do something*)."

guy: man
hanging around: spending time
suspiciously: strangely

to Have Something Up One's Sleeve

to have a secret idea or plan

- **He's always got something up his sleeve.** Right when we think we won't be able to make something work, *he thinks of a new way of doing it.*

- "Now **what have you got up your sleeve** (*what are you planning*)?"
  "Well, I'm thinking of a really good prank for April Fool's Day."

prank: trick or joke

to Be Game

to be willing to try or do something; to be okay

• "Let's play a game of chess while we're waiting. **Are you game?**"
"Sure. *I'm willing to try.* But don't get upset when I win."

• "How about going to a movie tonight?"
"Sure, **I'm game** (*that's okay with me*). Can we go to the early show?"

upset: unhappy

You're On

to accept your challenge/deal or
to indicate it's your turn

- "I bet you can't run to the corner in fifteen seconds."
  "**You're on**! I can do it in even less time."
  "*It's a deal*, but if you lose you'll have to treat me to a hamburger at lunch."

- "I bet I can beat you at this video game."
  "**You're on**! (*I accept your challenge*)."
  "What do I get if I win?"
  "Nothing."
  "Forget it!"

I bet: I'm going to guess that
to treat me to: to pay for

11

to Take a Crack at Something

to try doing or solving something

- Has anyone **taken a crack** at that algorithm? Even the world's best mathematicians seem afraid *to try doing it.*

- "I can't figure out what the problem is with this water heater. Can you **take a crack at it** (*solve the problem*)?" "Sure! I don't mind checking it out."

algorithm: an ordered set of mathematical rules for solving a problem
checking it out: looking at it

to Head Out

to get (start) going somewhere

- Let's all **head out** to the mall. We can take my car—there's a big one-day sale going on so we need *to get going!*

- We'd better **head out** (*start going*) before it rains. I've got a bad cold and I don't want to make it worse by getting wet.

Let's
Blow This Joint

let's get out of here; let's leave

- "I don't feel like sticking around this abandoned
  warehouse much longer. **Let's blow this joint** before
  the roof caves in."
  "I agree. *I'm ready to get out of here!*"

- It's way too loud and crowded in here! **Let's blow this
  joint** (*let's leave*) and go somewhere more quiet.

sticking around: waiting around
caves in: suddenly falls

to Knock It Off

to abruptly ask someone to stop doing something

- Hey, **knock it off**! We're trying to get the baby to sleep, so *stop turning up the music*!

- All right, **knock it off** (*stop laughing*). I'm serious about inventing an electric foot shaver. There's a huge market for beach bums with hairy feet!

beach bum: a person who doesn't work and always goes to the beach

to Stick Up for Someone

to say something in someone's defense

- Everyone questions Serge's reckless business ideas, but I always **stick up for him**. I *defend him* by pointing out his past successes.

- Although the coach told Kate that she wasn't good enough for the softball team, her friends **stuck up for her** (*came to her defense*). They told the coach they would give Kate extra practice on the weekends to help her improve.

reckless: careless or dangerous

Wrap It Up

it's time to quit; let's finish

- You two haven't finished gift-wrapping her presents yet? Come on! Let's **wrap it up**! We need *to finish* before she gets here and the party starts!

- **Wrap it up** (*it's time to quit*)! The foreman is coming and he won't appreciate the fact that we are playing poker on the job; we should be working!

come on: go faster
appreciate: understand the importance of something
poker: a card game usually played to win money

Section 2

Keep Your Pants On

Idioms for a hectic life

to Take a Rain Check

to decide to do at a later time; to reschedule plans for a future time

- "Did you go to the beach with your friend yesterday?"
  "Nope. We **took a rain check on that outing**. The weather was bad so we're *going to go at a later time*."

- "I'm sorry I can't go shopping with you today. How about **taking a rain check** (*making plans for another time*)?"
  "That's fine. I'll be counting on it."

be counting on it: be waiting for it

to Be Tied Up

to be busy or have no time; to have prior obligations, commitments, or things to do

- With Kenji's music lesson on Monday, Ana's soccer practice on Tuesday, Joey's parent-teacher conference on Wednesday, and my doctor's appointment on Thursday, **I'm all tied up**. I'm afraid *I have no time* to go grocery shopping until next week!

- "Unfortunately, the members of the management team **will be all tied up** (*have too many things to do*) this afternoon. Is it okay if you meet with the group tomorrow morning?"
"Sure, that will work out fine with me."

work out fine: be okay

to Be
Over One's Head

to be involved in something that is too much or too difficult to do, to finish, or to understand

- Her current workload **is completely over her head**. We need to get her an assistant or it will simply be *too much for her to finish*.

- The professor's explanation on quantum physics was way **over the heads of** (*too difficult to understand for*) his students who were just starting the class.

quantum physics: the theory of the structure and behavior of atoms and molecules

to Not Have a Clue

to have no idea about what's going on; to not know anything about something

- I'm always missing socks when I do the laundry. I **don't have a clue** what happens to them; *I've no idea where they go!*

- "What happened to Peter? He was walking with the group but I don't see him now."
  "**We don't have a clue** (*we have no idea where he might be*)."

Beats Me

to not be able to imagine why; to not know

- "Do you have any idea why they left in such a hurry?"
  "**Beats me**. They must not like our cooking very much. *I can't imagine any other reason why* they would run out of here like that."

- "How could he think that the situation would be solved by violence?"
  "**Beats me** (*I don't know*). I feel like violence just encourages more violence."

encourages: increases the possibility of

to Be Stumped

to not be able to answer a question; to be confused or puzzled; to have no more ideas

- **"I'm stumped on this question.** Just when was the battle fought and who won it?"
  "*I don't know the answer.* Let's look it up in the encyclopedia."

- His teachers **are stumped** (*puzzled*) by his brilliance. He never used to do his homework and now he's at the top of his class. What a refreshing change!

battle: a fight in a war
look it up: find the answer
refreshing: wonderful

to Be Done

to not tolerate (not accept) something; to not put up with someone/something anymore

- Her table manners are terrible! We're **done with her** unless she changes her behavior. We simply *won't tolerate her* slurping her soup and feeding turkey off the table to the dog.

- "**I'm totally done with** (*I will not put up with*) this computer. It's too slow and I can't get the Internet to function properly."
  "I believe you! That model is from the 1980s!"

slurping: eating noisily

27

to Be Beat

to be exhausted

- "Wow. Your desk is a mess! Are you okay?"
  "No, **I'm really beat**! I've done hours of work, and *I'm so tired I can hardly move.*"

- They were so **beat** (*exhausted*) from the flight to their friend's hometown for his wedding that they fell asleep during the ceremony.

a mess: cluttered or dirty

Cannot Hack It

***to not be able to take doing something; to not
be able to deal with the pressure of doing something; to not be able to keep up with something***

- She **can't hack** the long train commute. It normally
takes her over five hours to get to and from work every
day. She's finally decided she just *can't take it* anymore
and is going to find a job closer to home.

- Although Ilya's an amazing policeman, he **couldn't
hack it** (*couldn't deal with the pressure of it*) trying to
save people's lives everyday. He ultimately had a
nervous breakdown.

commute: trip made by one who travels every day to work

to Be Burned Out

to not be able to go on or take any more;
to become ineffective

- Poor guy. He's had so many problems at work that **he's all burned out**. He really needs to take a break since *he feels that he can't go on.*

- After trying to make the Olympic swim team five times, she felt **burned out** (*she couldn't keep on going any longer*) so she started playing golf instead.

to take a break: to temporarily stop doing something

to Be On Edge

to be nervous; to be irritable

- Saul was **on edge** right before his flu shot. He felt *quite nervous and was somewhat irritable.* He's always had a fear of needles.

- I don't blame her for being **on edge** (*nervous*). They want her to give a presentation in front of 500 of the world's most successful business people!

irritable: easily annoyed or angry

to Get
Carried Away

to get too involved in something; to do or use too much because of excitement/interest

- He **got carried away** on Ebay and ended up bidding on a massive stuffed bear. Funny how people can *get so involved* with buying junk.

- I'm warning you! Don't **get carried away** (*use too much*) when applying that self-tanning lotion. You'll turn orange!

ended up bidding: finally bid
stuffed: filled with material
self-tanning lotion: lotion used to make your skin tan (darker) without the sun

to Get
Out of Hand

*to lose control (get out of control) of a situation;
to not behave appropriately or to act wildly*

- "Trying to shop at that grocery store **gets out of hand**; there are way too many people and everyone rushes to get the ripest fruit first."
  "I agree. The whole thing *gets out of control!*"

- Alright, so sometimes my practical jokes **get out of hand** (*are not appropriate*). The other day I convinced Terri that the wasabi on her plate was avocado. I think her face turned green when she spooned it into her mouth. I feel awful!

ripest: the most ready to be eaten
wasabi: a Japanese condiment

to Fly
Off the Handle

to become so angry that you lose control; to lose one's temper

- Bill **flew off the handle** when the stewardess served him steak. We knew he was a vegetarian, but we didn't expect him to *become so angry*. After all, she was just serving the same dinner to all the passengers.

- Understandably, the woman **flew off the handle** (*became very angry*) when her car was hit from behind.

vegetarian: a person who does not eat any meat

to Freak Out

to shock, to disorient; to lose control

- Maria **freaked out** when the strange man proposed to her. She didn't know what to do and totally *lost it.*

- Hey! Don't **freak out** (*lose control*) on me now. Our performance is starting in one minute!

proposed: asked her to marry him

to Be Pissed Off

(vulgar)
to be angry

- Carlos always **pissed off** his classmates by scratching his fingernails on the board. It always *angered* them!

- When she saw her boyfriend with another girl, Jenny got so **pissed off** (*angry*) that she started screaming!

scratching his fingernails: making a scraping noise

to Blow Up

to yell at someone; to have a loud verbal exchange; to have an angry confrontation

- Suejin was finally convinced to calm down after she **blew up** at her secretary because he misplaced some mail. She *yelled* at him in front of the entire office!

- "What was all that hollering and screaming?
  "I **blew up** (*had an angry confrontation*) with the gardener. He let all my plants die while I was on vacation."

to Go Bananas

to get very excited; to go crazy

- The race car driver **went bananas** when he won. It's no wonder he *got so excited;* he broke a world record!

- They **totally went bananas** (*went crazy with excitement*) when they won dinner for two at the best restaurant in New York City.

broke a world record: did better than anyone else in the world

to Go Off the Deep End

to act irrationally (without control);
to be incredibly angry (livid)

- Okay, so you **went off the deep end** when Raz lost your snorkel. Why did you *act so irrationally?* After all, you found it in time to go on your scuba-diving trip.

- Ayumi would **go off the deep end** (*be incredibly angry*) if her husband ever sold her grand piano to buy a new big-screen TV.

snorkel: vertical tube used to breathe under water
scuba-diving: the sport of swimming under water while breathing from a container of air on your back

39

to Hit the Ceiling

to not be able to take it; to not take any more stress; to become very angry

- I'm about **to hit the ceiling**—there is way too much noise in this library! *I can't take it anymore!*

- My dad **hit the ceiling** (*became extremely angry*) when he saw me pull into the driveway with his brand new Mercedes. I really don't blame him; I had gotten in an accident and the car's windshield had gotten shattered.

pull into the driveway: arrive
brand new: completely new; never used before
shattered: broken into small pieces

to Be Trippin'

to be crazy; to be thinking strange thoughts

- "He must **be trippin'**. When he woke up this morning,
  he said the sky was green."
  "*Is he crazy?* There's no way the sky could have been
  green. That plane flight must have done something to
  his brain."

- "Where do you want to go for dinner?"
  "Yeah. The lighting does seem dimmer."
  "**Are you trippin'**? (*Are you thinking strange thoughts?*) I
  asked you if you wanted to go to dinner."
  "Oh! I thought I heard 'the lighting does seem dimmer.'"

dimmer: less bright

41

to Be
Out of Whack

to be crazy or irrational; to need adjustment

- "He is completely **out of whack** with reality. He thinks money grows on trees."
  "I agree—he's always seemed *irrational* when talking about finances."

- What's wrong here? My car won't start. Something **is out of whack** (*needs adjusting*).

irrational: not in control

to Get a Grip

to stay focused; to control oneself

- He needs to **get a grip** and *control himself.* It's not the end of the world just because he's bad at arm wrestling.

- Sure, you didn't get invited to Elham's party, but stop moaning about it and **get a grip** (*try to control your emotions*)! Even if your feelings are hurt, remember that other special occasions are coming up and I know you'll be invited!

arm wrestling: a contest that tests the arm strength of two competitors
moaning: complaining

to Hang In There

to work something through; to be patient

- "Wow! There's so much left to paint; I don't see how I'll ever finish!"
  "**Hang in there**. I'll bring a brush and help you. *Just be patient and everything will work out okay.*"

- **Hang in there** (*be patient; the situation will improve*). Even though your team is down by two goals with five minutes remaining, they could still win.

down by: in a lower or inferior position

to Lay Off

to stop indulging oneself; to leave someone alone or to stop bothering someone

- If you want to lose weight, you'd better **lay off** all that stew you keep gulping down. Retiring from sumo wrestling is going to require that you *stop eating (indulging in food) so much.*

- I'm going to dunk her into the swimming pool if she doesn't **lay off** (*stop*) reminding me to wear sunscreen!

gulping down: eating large amounts rapidly or greedily
dunk: put someone/something under water for a very short time
sunscreen: a lotion used to protect your skin from the ultraviolet rays of the sun

to Lighten Up

to stop being so serious or demanding; to be less rough or rude with someone

- The children would clean up their toys if the babysitter would **lighten up on them.** She needs *to be less demanding.*

- **Lighten up** (*don't be so rough*) on Arthur! He didn't mean to get lost downtown; he just hates asking for directions!

demanding: requiring careful attention or constant effort

to Give Someone a Break

to not be so demanding or harsh;
to not believe someone

- "She's trying to learn how to walk on hot coals, but she hasn't mastered the technique yet; it's taking her forever!" "**Give her a break.** *Let's not be so demanding!* You know it's not easy."

- You said you got a perfect score on your biology exam? And you didn't even study for it? **Give me a break**! (*You don't really expect me to believe that, do you?*)

Taking Care of Business

Idioms for assuming responsibility

to Call the Shots

to decide what is to be done; to be
in charge of a situation

- "Now that she's been appointed manager, I guess she'll be **calling the shots**."
  "That's great! I can't think of anyone more qualified *to make all the decisions* around here.

- Do you really think we can repair this wreck of a boat? Since I don't know anything about fixing boats, you should **call the shots** (*be in charge of the situation*).

wreck of a boat: greatly damaged boat

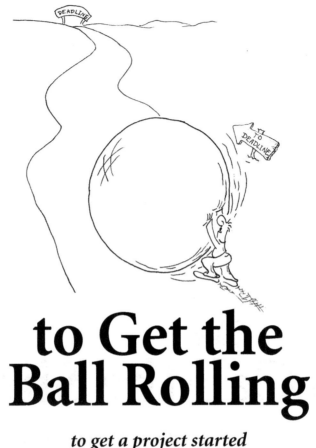

to Get the Ball Rolling

to get a project started

- Everyone, let's pay attention to this project! We only have one month to complete it, so **let's get the ball rolling**. *We've got to start working on it* as quickly as possible.

- All you have to do is **get the ball rolling** (*start working on the project*), and we'll do the rest. That's what friends are for!

to Start
From Scratch

to begin a project composed of the basics/original material; to start from nothing at all

- My dad loves to bake and always **starts from scratch**. He never uses the cake mix that you can buy in a box. He *begins by using the basic ingredients*: flour, sugar, and a few eggs.

- That woman's a genius. She started her online business **from scratch** (*from nothing at all*) and built it up to a multimillion-dollar enterprise.

a genius: very smart/intelligent
enterprise: a business company

to Pull
Something Off

*to succeed in doing something difficult
or unexpected*

- "That's a really great idea. Do you think you can
  pull it off?"
  "If all goes well, I'll convince my wife that this striped
  wallpaper is better than flowery wallpaper. *It might be
  difficult but I believe I'll succeed!*"

- His friends told him he'd never be able to open his
  own store, but through careful planning and support
  from the bank **he pulled it off** (*he unexpectedly
  succeeded*).

convince my wife: give my wife good reasons
wallpaper: paper for decorating walls

to Give It a Go/Shot/Whirl

to try something

- You've never been on a roller coaster? Why not **give it a go** and see if you like it? It's really exciting—you should *try it.* Don't be afraid.

- Come on! **Let's give it a shot** (*let's try it*). We just might get a prize if we enter that dance competition. We've got a good routine and we look great together.

roller coaster: a curved track that people ride on for fun
routine: series of dance steps

55

to Take the Heat

to receive or put up with criticism
for something

- Don't worry. I'll **take the heat** for forgetting to lock the door. I should have remembered it and *deserve all the criticism* I get.

- Joaquin **couldn't take the heat** (*couldn't put up with the criticism*) at his previous job, but he's doing much better with his new one.

to Go to Bat for Someone

to give help or support to someone who is in trouble

- "You really **went to bat for me** when you convinced the boss to lighten my workload. I can't thank you enough for having *helped me*."

- "Hi, Ruby. What's new?"
  "Well, I'm feeling a little disappointed because someone else got the lead in the school play."
  "Have faith. I'll **go to bat for you** (*support you*) any day. Your musical and dancing skills are phenomenal."

convinced the boss: gave the boss good reasons
lighten: decrease
lead: main part/role
have faith: it'll be okay
phenomenal: really good

to Come Clean

to be truthful about something (especially when it is not expected of the person); to admit doing something wrong

- Moua, **come clean** and *tell me the truth*. Did you skip school today?

- All right, who set the fire alarm off at midnight? Someone needs **to come clean** (*to be truthful*) about it or you'll all be getting in trouble.

skip: not go to
getting in trouble: getting punished for doing something wrong

to Fill Someone In

to let someone know the details about something; to give someone a detailed explanation about something

- Please **fill me in** on what was said at the town meeting. I want to make sure I vote for the best policy and it would help if you *let me know the details of the discussion.*

- Don't forget **to fill Jessie in** (*to give Jessie a complete explanation*) on the fact that Lee's party is supposed to be a surprise. Otherwise, I'm sure he'll tell her all about it!

to Be No Big Deal

to not matter much or not be very important or serious; to not be troublesome or difficult to do something

- It's **no big deal** if he stays in the casino. He only gambles with pennies, hence any loss of money *won't be a serious one!*

- "You think it **won't be a big deal** (*won't be troublesome*) to clean out the garage?"
  "Nope. Most of that junk can go directly to the dump."

casino: a place where people try to win money by playing games
hence: therefore; for this reason
junk: useless things
dump: a big place for everyone's garbage

to Be a
Piece of Cake

to be very easy to do

- "Can you help me fasten this leg to the stool?"
  "Sure, **it's a piece of cake**. Just hold the stool so it
  doesn't move, and I'll fasten the leg in place. *It's really
  very easy.*"

- Learning to speak a new language **is no piece of cake**
  (*is not easy to do*) for me. I wish it came more naturally!

stool: a seat with no back or arms
fasten: attach

to Get
the Hang of (It)

to get an understanding of doing something through experience; to learn the skills/knowledge to do something correctly

- This power drill will make our lives so much easier as soon as I **get the hang of it**. It's a highly advanced model, hence it'll take a while *to understand how to use it.*

- She's only been working at the library for a week, but she knows where every book is—she **got the hang of it quickly** (*learned what to do quickly*).

hence: therefore; for this reason
power drill: a motorized tool for making holes in something

to Nail Something (Down)

to do something correctly or perfectly; to get something just right

- Class, we've been practicing these multiplication tables for a long time. With a little more work you can **nail them down**. For homework tonight go over them until you *remember all of them correctly.*

- You completely **nailed it** (*got it right*) when you predicted that the Internet would become our preferred mode of communication in the future.

multiplication tables: a table listing certain numbers multiplied together and their answers
predicted: guessed it would happen before it happened
preferred: favorite1
mode: type

to Put (Something) On the Back Burner

to delay doing something temporarily; to give something a low priority

- They desperately need my help in the restaurant; it looks like we'll have to **put our trip to visit your family on the back burner**. Hopefully we'll only have to *delay the trip temporarily*.

- Your ideas for renovating the bathroom are great, but we'll need to **put them on the back burner** (*give them low priority*). There are just too many other important things that need fixing in the house first.

desperately need: greatly need
renovating: improving

to Cough Up

to give something; to hand something over; to come up with something

- You better **cough up** some spare change if you expect me to take your muddy clothes to the Laundromat. I'll only do it if you *give me* enough quarters for the machine.

- If you want to join the group going to China this summer, you've got to **cough up** (*come up with*) the first payment for the tour by the deadline.

spare change: extra/additional coins
muddy: dirty
deadline: last possible day to do it

Let the Good Times Roll

Idioms for good fortune

Way to Go

to congratulate; to say good job/it's a good job

- "I just received a scholarship to an art institute in Milan, Italy!"

  "Wow! **Way to go**! You deserve it. *Congratulations!*"

- "The English teachers' conference is being held here this summer. Are you going?"

  "I wouldn't miss it! In fact, I'll be making a presentation on my new book. People have told me they think it's the ultimate idiom resource."

  "**Way to go** (*that's wonderful; good for you*)!"

  you deserve it: you should get it (because you've done a good job)
  ultimate: best
  resource: reference book

to Have It Made

to be in a desirable position; to have everything you want; to have succeeded

- "Have you seen the car Alexa is driving?"
  " Yeah! She's **had it made** ever since she got that new job as a test driver. She'll never have to drive an old car again; in fact, she'll be able to *get any car she wants!*"

- The Salvoldis were smart to have bought that house at such a reasonable price. Now they've **got it made** (*are in an extremely desirable position*) since the value of the house has more than doubled.

---

test driver: a driver who drives a car to evaluate its performance
reasonable: good/fair

to Have
a Blast/Ball

to have lots of fun; to have a great time

- Celebrating the Fourth of July **is a blast.** *It's so much fun* to gather friends and family, barbeque, and watch the fireworks!

- "Where did you guys go on spring break?"
  "We went to Cancun. We **had an absolute ball** (*had a great time*)."
  "What did you do for an entire week?"
  "We lounged on the beach every day and partied every night!"

barbeque: to cook food over a fire
lounged: relaxed

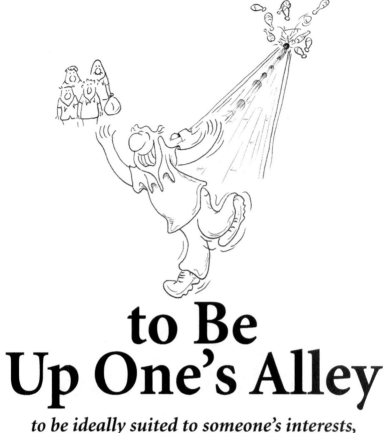

to Be
Up One's Alley

to be ideally suited to someone's interests,
skills, or abilities; to be your interest/preference

- Bowling is **right up your alley**. *You are incredibly skilled* at it.

- That style of clothing is **not up your alley** (*not suited for you*); you just don't look good in ruffles and polka dots.

ruffles: folds of cloth
polka dots: a pattern of dots

to Be On a Roll

to get more successful quickly; to be constantly succeeding; to have a series of successes

- First every deli in the city wanted his recipe for mustard; then pesto; now they want his recipe for vinaigrette. He's **on a roll** with his condiments business; it just keeps *getting more successful!*

- Wow! You found three antique clocks at the flea market this past week? You're really **on a roll** (*having a series of successes*) with your collection.

condiments: items used to flavor food
antique: over 100 years old
flea market: market selling old and used items

73

to Be Sweet

to be really good; to be great

- We just bought a 152-inch plasma TV, and I've got to say **it's sweet**. The clarity and definition of the picture *is really good.*

- That's one **sweet** (*great*) suitcase! The neon plaid print will certainly make it easy to find at the baggage claim.

plasma TV: a high-technology TV
neon: bright, electrifying
plaid: pattern of squares

to Be Tight

to be wonderful; to be impressive

- That 360-twist flip on your snowboard **was really tight**! In fact, it *was so impressive* that you should consider competing in the Extreme Snowboarding Competition.

- The video game I got for Christmas **is really tight** (*is really great*). I could play it 24/7.

360-twist flip: complete circle in the air
24/7: 24 hours a day, seven days a week

to Be Hot

to be fantastic; to be popular and attractive at the moment

- Have you heard that young pianist from Japan? **He's hot!** In fact, *he's such a fantastic player* that his concerts sell out the minute tickets go on sale.

- That new reality TV show **is hot** (*is so popular*). Everyone's watching it!

sell out: have no more tickets to sell
reality TV: TV shows featuring "ordinary" people, not actors

to Be
Hooked (On)

to not be able to stop doing something;
to be addicted to something

- "I can't get this jingle on the radio out of my head. **I'm totally hooked on** it."
  "*You really can't make it stop?* Let's try singing a song— but then a song might get stuck in your head too!"

- Poor Angelina **is so hooked on** (*is so addicted to*) Broadway that she's still auditioning for a part after twenty years of trying.

jingle: advertising rhyme
get stuck: not go away
Broadway: a street in New York City where famous theaters are located

to Hook
Someone Up

to get someone to meet someone else; to get something that someone really wants

- Let me **hook you up with** a friend of mine. I'm convinced you'll fall in love with her once *you meet her!*

- I can **hook you up** (*get you what you want*) if you have enough cash to buy it. An eighteenth-century chandelier isn't cheap nor easy to find!

chandelier: a fancy frame that holds lights and hangs from the ceiling

to Hit
On Someone

to flirt with someone; to make
a pass at someone

- A lot of the men at the party were **hitting on her**—she looked so good in that dress. However, since Sharmin prefers to be single, she paid no attention to the men *flirting with her.*

- They know that Isaac would make a fun partner in a relationship, so it's no wonder they are always **hitting on him** (*flirting with him*).

to Dig (Someone or Something)

to like someone/something a lot

- The children **really dig playing in the sandbox**; we take them to the park every Sunday and they spend hours in the sand—*they sure like doing that a lot!*

- "Have you listened to that CD I let you borrow?" "Yeah! **I dig it** (*I like it a lot*)! I'm going to download it right now."

download: get it from the computer

to Knock
Someone Dead

to greatly impress someone with an outstanding performance or display

- Don't be nervous. You're going **to knock them dead** with your magic show. When they see how you make the rabbit appear out of your hat, there is no doubt that *everyone will be impressed!*

- He looks great! He'll **knock 'em dead** (*greatly impress people*) when they see him in that designer outfit.

designer outfit: clothing made by a famous person(s) in the fashion industry

Knock Yourself Out

to have fun; to have a lot of something; to go ahead and do something really enjoyable; to indulge

- "That's a cool looking video game you've got there. Can I borrow it?"
  "Go right ahead! **Knock yourself out**! It's really challenging. *Have fun* trying to get to the last level."

- "This food is delicious! May I have more?"
  "Absolutely. **Knock yourself out** (*have as much as you want/indulge*)! You do know that's a sea slug, don't you?"

cool: great (slang)
sea slug: a marine animal related to the snail

to Die For

to think something is really wonderful/great

- "I've never had chocolates like these. They're **to die for**."
  "I agree. They're imported from Switzerland and they taste *absolutely wonderful*. Here—have some more."

- "They have three homes, a private jet, personal chefs—the works! Their lives are **to die for** (*are really great*)."
  "Hmm . . . I'm not sure I agree. Does money really buy happiness?"

the works: everything

to Rock

to do something really well; to be outstanding or superior

- How did you learn to play the guitar? **You really rock**! Did you have a teacher, or did you learn *to play so well* by yourself?

- The deal they're offering **totally rocks** (*is outstanding*)! For every pair of shoes you buy, you get a second pair for free!

What Happened?

Idioms for delivering bad news

to Blow It/Something

to carelessly spend money; to fail or have no possibility of a successful outcome; to lose an opportunity

- "What are you going to do with all the money you won?"
  "I'm going **to blow it** on jewelry for my girlfriend."
  "Really? Are you sure you should *carelessly spend it* like that?"

- She really **blew it** (*failed*) when she washed her red underwear with his white work shirts. His clothes are completely ruined.

to Do a Number On Someone/Something

to cause hurt; to damage or harm someone or something

- "That guy's not very nice. He **did a number on** Julie when he failed to show up for his date with her without calling. He *deeply hurt her feelings.*"

- "Did you see Yasuf's car after the accident?"
  "Yah. Someone **did a real number on it** (*damaged it quite extensively*). It was completely totaled."

totaled: destroyed

to Be Wasted

to be drunk; to have an altered mindset;
to not be sober

- "Let's buy some beer and **get wasted**!"
  "No thanks. I really shouldn't *get drunk* tonight. It wouldn't be a great idea for me to go to work hung over tomorrow morning."

- I don't know what substance she took, but she **was totally wasted** (*had an altered mindset*). By the time the police showed up she was unconscious on the sidewalk.

hung over: with a headache from drinking too much alcohol
had an altered mindset: was not thinking clearly
unconscious: in a state like a deep sleep

to Be Busted

to be caught in the act of doing something secretive or illegal; to be in trouble

- The robber **got busted** for attempting to steal the prized statue from the art gallery. He should've known he'd *get caught doing such an illegal act!*

- Every night the child said he ate his peas, but he was actually hiding them under the cushion of his chair. He **got busted** (*got in trouble*) when his mom decided to clean the cushions.

cushion: bag filled with soft material

to Be Caught Red-Handed

to be caught in the act of doing something bad or illegal

- Don't act like you didn't do it. **I caught you red-handed** eating half of that cake before dinner time. *I saw you and you've been a bad boy.*

- The thief **was caught red-handed** (*was caught in the act*). A pedestrian saw him trying to break the window of my car and called the police.

pedestrian: a person walking by

to Get Ripped Off/
to Be a Rip Off

to get cheated; to pay more than one should have;
to be too expensive

- Everyone thinks they're buying designer jeans at a low price from that website, but really **the jeans are a rip off**. The jeans have fake labels and hence *everyone buying them is getting cheated!*

- We realized that **we had gotten ripped off** (*paid more than we should have*) when we found the same furniture in another store for half the price! Next time we'll visit more stores before we decide to buy.

fake: not real

to Get the Short End of the Stick

to get the less desirable part or amount of something; to get the least favorable outcome

- Why am I always **getting the short end of the stick**? I contribute just as much as my roommates in the house, yet I'm always the one who *has to do the undesirable task* of cleaning the bathroom. It's not fair.

- He **got the short end of the stick** (*got the least favorable outcome*) when he had to stay home and babysit the kids while his wife went out to a party.

to Have
a Falling Out

to stop communicating with someone due to an argument or disagreement; to damage your relationship with someone

- Ramona and Raquel **had a falling out** over their grandmother's will. They both wanted her jewelry, but their grandmother left all the jewelry for Ramona. Both sisters *stopped talking to each other* for years.

- "Hey, Minh—I thought you were at work at this time of day. What are you doing here?"
  "**I had a falling out** (*I damaged my relationship*) with my boss this morning. She made me so mad. I'm never going back there."

to Have a Bone to Pick with Someone

to want to talk to someone about something they've done that is annoying/upsetting

- "Ignacio, stop leaving your dirty dishes all over the place!"

  "Look! If **you've got a bone to pick with me** about my messiness, why don't you get maid service?"

  "I first *need you to know how annoying it is* to live like this."

- I **have a bone to pick with Amelia** (*there is something upsetting that I need to talk about*). Why does she always make so much noise when she comes home late at night?

messiness: dirty and disorganized habits
how annoying it is: how angry it makes me

to Have It
In for Someone

to constantly blame someone; to dislike everything someone does, regardless of the outcome

- The teacher really **had it in for Hillary**. He *constantly blamed her* for disturbing the class, even when it wasn't her fault.

- Maria has **had it in for Roger** (*dislikes Roger*) ever since he left a tub of ice cream melting on her new suede couch. She ignores all his phone calls!

blamed her: made her responsible
disturbing: making noise in
tub: container
suede: leather

to Let
Someone Have It

to attack someone verbally;
to lecture someone in anger

- My dad really **let me have it** the other night for coming in way past my curfew. He *very angrily told me* that I'd lose my allowance and all driving privileges for a whole week.

- Our teacher really **let us have it** (*lectured us in anger*) for not turning in our homework. He made us each write an essay on the importance of completing our work on time.

curfew: a law enforcing someone to be home (indoors) at a certain time (often dictated by a parent to his/her child)
allowance: money given at regular intervals

to Give Someone a Hard Time

to cause trouble and unnecessary difficulty for somebody

- The boss **gave him a hard time** at work for being late; in fact, the boss *gave him so much trouble* that he just quit.

- Stop **giving me a hard time** (*giving me all this trouble*)! I'm scared of heights and nothing you say is going to convince me to climb to the top of that tower!

scared of: frightened of
tower: tall, narrow buidling

to Throw In the Towel

to stop trying; to give up

- After climbing a mountain, kayaking two rivers, and bicycling 50 miles, Marci had **to throw in the towel** during the final stage of the endurance competition. She was simply too exhausted and had *to stop*.

- I'm about ready **to throw in the towel** (*to give up*). I've tried everything to get along with my son and he tries everything to shock me, from his green hair to his full-body tattoo!

kayaking: a sport in which people go down a river in a long, narrow boat
endurance: challenging how long one can last
to get along with: to have a friendly relationship with
shock: upset

to Shake Up Someone

to upset someone

- "He was pretty **shaken up** by the accident."
  "It would **upset** me too if I were driving and someone hit my car going 60 miles per hour!"

- The events of September 11th **shook up** (*upset*) the entire world.

to Give It to Someone Straight

to say something directly and honestly

- Let me **give it to you straight**: because of your lack of expertise in mechanical engineering, we won't be able to hire you for the job. We're just *letting you know the exact reasons.*

- I'll **give it to you straight** (*tell you directly and honestly*). We aren't going to use your office-cleaning services because you charge too much!

lack of: absence of
expertise: expert (specialized) knowledge

to Be a Bummer

to be a bad or difficult situation;
to be disappointing

- **It was a huge bummer** when her car broke down. It really put her in *a difficult situation.*

- When I went to see my dentist he told me that I had three cavities. **What a bummer** (*how very disappointing*). I guess I'll have to start flossing!

to Be
Bummed Out

to be feeling bad; to be discouraged
or depressed

- "We've got to do something to cheer Liz up."
  "What's going on?"
  "She's **bummed out** because the rabbits chewed up her dolls."
  "I don't blame her. I'd *feel bad* too. Why not take her out for ice cream? That should make her feel better."

- They were **all bummed out** (*discouraged*) when they tried to get tickets for the show and discovered there were no more available.

chewed up: ate

103

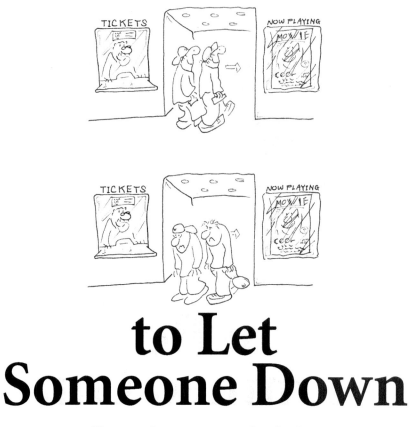

to Let Someone Down

to disappoint someone by failing to perform or meet their expectations

- Dude, that movie really **let me down**. I was expecting more high-speed chases and less kissing scenes. *It was truly disappointing.*

- There's no way I can vote for your candidate. I don't mean to **let you down** (*to disappoint you*), but when she was elected before she always made the wrong decisions.

dude: slang for a person, typically a male
high-speed chases: a car(s) following fast and close to catch another car

to Be a Drag

to be undesirable, boring,
troublesome, or uninteresting

• "You don't look so good. Didn't you just get back from
summer camp?"
"Yeah, I got back yesterday, but the camp **was a real
drag**. All we did was study the habits of insects all day;
it *got incredibly boring*. I wasted my time there."

• "How come you quit your job?"
"It **was a drag** (*was totally uninteresting*). The only thing I
did was seal envelopes eights hours a day."
"That's so tedious! I hope you find a better job!"

habits: repeated actions
wasted my time: did not use my time in a meaningful way
tedious: boring; tiresome

to Suck

(vulgar)
to be awful, terrible, or no good at all

- It **sucks** to go hiking in that part of the forest. You have to watch where you step the whole time because there's quicksand everywhere. An outing like that is simply *no fun*.

- "What did you think of last night's football game?"
  "It was a real disappointment. Our team **sucked** (*was really bad*). The players were completely overcome by the opposing team's defense."

  to go hiking: to go on a long walk in the wilderness
  quicksand: wet sand that is dangerous because it pulls you down
  overcome: controlled
  defense: part of the team that stops the other team from scoring in a game

to Mess/Screw Up

("screw" is informal/potentially vulgar)
to not do something correctly or to make mistakes; to do or say something wrong

- Oh no, I **screwed up**! This recipe says we need to add powdered sugar. I added cornstarch! I can't believe I *made this mistake!*

- "How did his job interview go?"
  "Mostly okay, but **he messed up** (*said the wrong thing*) when he told us his previous boss thought he was lazy."
  "Wow! That's definitely the wrong thing to say in an interview!"

cornstarch: a flour used in cooking to make liquids thicker

to Be Screwed

(vulgar)
to be in a lot of trouble; to get cheated

- "**I'm so screwed**! There's no way I can clean the house before my parents get here."
  "It was your idea to have a big party. *You're in so much trouble* I feel sorry for you."

- The basketball team felt like they'd been **screwed** (*cheated*) when the referee called the foul on their team; it was obvious that a player on the other team had pushed their player.

foul: something done against the rules

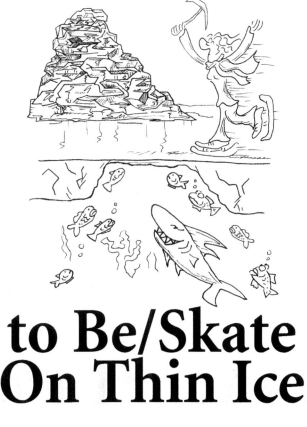

to Be/Skate
On Thin Ice

to be close to getting into trouble;
to be in a risky situation

- I'm warning you; you're **skating on thin ice** if you think you can climb that glacier. Don't *put yourself in such a risky situation.*

- As the chief executive officer of Parachutes Incorporated, he can't afford **to skate on thin ice** (*risk getting himself into a troublesome situation*). All of his decisions need to be made cautiously and carefully.

glacier: a large mass of ice

In Your Face

to be right and abruptly let someone else know they're wrong

- I'm right! It is your turn to take out the trash. You swore the schedule read differently. *You're wrong.* **In your face!**

- **In your face** (*you were wrong*)! I knew you couldn't drink that expired quart of milk without getting sick!

swore (past tense of swear): seriously promised
expired: no longer okay to use/drink

to Chicken Out (On)

to choose not to do or try something because of fear

- They were all set to go to the museum with some friends, but at the last minute they **chickened out**. They *chose not to go because they're scared* of the dinosaur exhibit. Apparently seeing such things gives them nightmares.

- **Don't chicken out on** (*Don't decide not to try*) going whitewater rafting. We know it can be dangerous, but you'll be with a group of professional guides!

whitewater rafting: a sport in which people go down a very fast moving river in a simple boat

111

Section 6
That's Life
Idioms for everything else

What's Up (with Somebody)?

a casual/informal way to say "what are you doing?";
What's going on?/What's happening?/What's wrong?

- "**What's up**, Jeremy?"
  "Not much; I'm just getting some errands done."
  "I have a lot of errands to do as well. *What are you doing* this evening?"

- "**What's up** (*what's wrong*) with Mr. Jones? Ever since he came back from his trip to the Amazon he's been acting strange. I hardly recognize him anymore."
  "I've noticed that too. Maybe he caught some type of illness in the jungle."

errands: short trips to do things

to Chill Out

to take it easy; to be patient; to not get excited

- Wouldn't it be nice to just **chill out** on a tropical beach for a few months eating grapes and caviar? I really need to *take it easy* after all this work.

- Hey, Joan, **chill out** (*take it easy*). Everything is going to be okay despite the dry cleaner misplacing your favorite dress.

caviar: the eggs of a fish (eaten as an appetizer)

to Tag Along

to follow after or go along with someone

• "Where are you going, mom?"
  "I'm just going for a short walk.
  "Can I **tag along**?"
  "Sure. *Follow me!*"

• "Wait up! I love window-shopping. Mind if I **tag along**
  (*go with you*)?
  "No problem. We love company. The more, the merrier."

window-shopping: looking at goods (through the store windows) but not buying them
the more, the merrier: it's better with more people

117

to Go Dutch

to each pay for his/her own meal when dining together; to split the cost or check

- "How was dinner at that new restaurant?"
  "Great! But it was somewhat pricey, so we all **went Dutch** and each person *paid for his own meal.*"

- Dale and Liz **always go Dutch** (*split the cost*) whenever they go to the opera.

pricey: expensive
split: divide

to Crash (Someplace)

to stay the night; to go to sleep

- "I'm too beat to make the drive home. Do you think I could **crash** at your place tonight?"
  "Sure! You can *sleep on the couch.* It's really no problem."

- Tania had to work the night shift for the entire week; she was so tired that she **crashed** (*went to sleep*) in the parking lot.

beat: tired
the night shift: between the hours of 9:00 pm and 5:00 am

119

to Mess/Screw Around

("screw" is informal/potentially vulgar)
to be involved in an unproductive activity and/or get nowhere; to waste time

- I need to stop **screwing around** with this motor. I know nothing about mechanics and I'm *getting nowhere* trying to fix this!

- Jorge **doesn't mess around** (*doesn't waste time*) in his new airport security job. He knows our safety depends on him!

to Keep In Touch

to keep some type of contact with someone you will no longer see on a regular basis

- Unfortunately, we're going to have to ask that you **keep in touch** during your vacation. If there's a crisis at work, we'll need *to contact you* immediately.

- "Sorry to see you go. Any idea how long you'll be gone?" "Hard to say, but I'll **keep in touch** (*be contacting you*) via email."

to Stick to One's Guns

to refuse to change your ideas or beliefs; to not change your mind

- If he's convinced that he's right, he should **stick to his guns**. He shouldn't allow himself to be intimidated by criticism and should *refuse to change his beliefs*.

- Don't let anybody tell you that you shouldn't take part in the peace demonstration. **Just stick to your guns** (*don't change your mind*).

he's convinced: he believes
intimidated: scared
refuse: not accept

No Way (José)

definitely not; not at all

- You want to walk through that haunted house at night?! **No way José!** Even if you paid me, *I wouldn't do it.*

- "Would you lend me your diamond necklace for the party?"
  "No way (*absolutely not*)! The last time I lent you jewelry, you dropped my earrings down the toilet!"

haunted house: a house where ghosts live

Screw That

("screw" is informal/potentially vulgar)
to reject something; to not accept something

- "How about driving to Los Angeles this weekend?"
  "**Screw that**! It's way too far to drive from New York City to Los Angeles in one weekend! *I'm rejecting that idea*—and don't even try to convince me otherwise."

- You expect me to go skydiving with you? **Screw that**! (*I'll never accept such an invitation!*) Skydiving is way too scary!

convince me otherwise: change what I think
skydiving: the sport of jumping from an airplane and falling through the sky
scary: frightening

Go Figure

it's hard to imagine; what else did you expect?

- "Someone told me that Brad was accepted to medical school."
  "We heard the same thing. **Go figure.** He can't even keep his houseplants alive; *it's hard to imagine* him being a doctor."

- "These customers are so hard to please! We give them discounts but that's not enough; we fly them to the Bahamas with all expenses paid, but that's not enough; now they're asking that we pay for their spa treatments!"
  "**Go figure** (*what else did you expect?*)."

spa treatments: relaxing bath services, often including massages

to Butt In

to interrupt; to get involved

- I'm sorry **to butt in,** but the boss is on the phone. He
  wants to speak with you. You know I would never want
  to interrupt unless it was really important!

- Pardon me for **butting in** (*interrupting your
  conversation*), but there's a fire downstairs!

to Rub It In

to make someone feel worse or jealous;
to criticize someone excessively

- I wanted to **rub it in** and *make everyone even
  more jealous,* so I told all my colleagues at work I'd be
  thinking of them as I cruise around the world on my
  lottery winnings.

- "Sorry you got stuck in the snow. Didn't you hear about
  the storm?"
  "I did. But I thought if I drove fast enough I'd get home
  before it hit."
  "That was not very smart of you."
  "I know—**don't rub it in** (*don't make me feel any worse
  than I already do*)."

That Cracks Me Up

that makes me laugh very hard

- **That cracks me up**. Could anyone else play a joke like that on the chief of police? The situations you get yourself into always *make me laugh*.

- Those campers **crack me up** (*make me laugh*). On a dare, they said they were going to sleep all night without a tent. The mosquitoes will eat them alive!

on a dare: for a challenge

Index to Idioms

A

a piece of cake *61*

B

ball's in your court *3*
be a bummer *102*
be a drag *105*
be a piece of cake *59*
be beat *28*
be bummed out *103*
be busted *90*
be caught red-handed *91*
be done *27*
be game *10*
be hooked (on) *77*
be hot *76*
be no big deal *60*
be on edge *31*
be on a roll *73*
be out of whack *42*
be over one's head *23*
be pissed off *36*
be screwed *108*
be/skate on thin ice *109*
be stumped *26*
be sweet *74*
be tied up *22*
be tight *75*
be trippin' *41*
be up one's alley *72*
be up to something *8*
be wasted *89*
beats me *25*
blow it/something *87*
blow this joint *14*
blow up *37*
bummed out *103*
bummer *102*
burned out *30*
butt in *126*

C

call the shots *51*
cannot hack it *29*
caught red-handed *91*
chicken out (on) *111*
chill out *116*
come clean *58*
cough up *65*
crash (someplace) *119*

D

die for *83*
dig (someone or
  something) *80*
do a number on someone/
  something *89*

F

fill someone in *59*
fly off the handle *34*
freak out *35*

G

get a grip *43*
get carried away *32*
get out of hand *33*
get ripped off/
  be a rip off *92*
get the ball rolling *52*
get the hang of it *62*
get the lead out *6*
get the short end of
  the stick *93*
get with it *5*
give it a go/shot/whirl *55*
give it to someone
  straight *101*
give someone a break *47*
give someone a
  hard time *98*

go bananas *38*
go dutch *118*
go figure *125*
go off the deep end *39*
go to bat for someone *57*

H

hang in there *44*
have a blast/ball *71*
have a bone to pick
  with someone *95*
have a falling out *94*
have it in for someone *96*
have it made *70*
have something up
  one's sleeve *9*
head out *13*
hit on someone *79*
hit the ceiling *40*
hook someone up *78*
hooked (on) *77*
hot *76*

I

in your face *110*

K

keep in touch *121*
knock it off *15*
knock someone dead *81*
knock yourself out *82*

L

lay off *45*
let someone down *104*
let someone have it *97*
let's blow this joint *14*
lighten up *46*

M

mess/screw around *120*
mess/screw up *107*

N

nail something (down) *63*
no big deal *60*
no way (José) *123*
not have a clue, *24*

O

on a roll *73*
on edge *31*
out of whack *42*
over one's head *23*

P

pissed *36*
pull something off *54*
put (something) on the
  back burner *64*

R

rock *84*
roll *4*
rub it in *127*

S

screw that *124*
screwed *108*
shake up someone *100*
skate on thin ice *109*
start from scratch *53*
stay on one's toes *7*
stick to one's guns *122*
stick up for someone *16*
stumped *26*
suck *106*
sweet *74*

T

tag along *117*
take a crack at
  something *12*
take a rain check *21*
take the heat *56*
that cracks me up *128*
throw in the towel *99*
tied up *22*
tight *75*
trippin' *41*

U

up one's alley *72*

W

wasted *89*
way to go *69*
what's up (with
  somebody) *115*
wrap it up *17*

Y

you're on *11*